Original title:
Oakwood Odes

Copyright © 2025 Creative Arts Management OÜ
All rights reserved.

Author: Elias Marchant
ISBN HARDBACK: 978-1-80567-206-7
ISBN PAPERBACK: 978-1-80567-505-1

Beneath the Canopy

Squirrels run fast, wearing their best,
A nutty competition, in their little vest.
The branches sway, a leafy crowd,
Cheering for acorns, all fun and loud.

Birds gossip high, in a ruffled choir,
Comically caught in a storm of desire.
Their tunes are silly, as if on cue,
A laughable show, just for me and you.

Time Stands Still

In this slow place, I lost my watch,
A chipmunk borrowed it, just to blotch.
Now hours drag like a snail on a spree,
Time giggles softly, just you and me.

Every tick-tock seems to mock my stride,
Nature's clock giggles, can't run and hide.
We'll dance in circles, giggle and squeal,
Who needs a schedule? Let's just feel!

Lullabies of the Leafy Knoll

Crickets play tunes, off-pitch and sweet,
Under the stars, a rhythmic heartbeat.
They hum lullabies, with a quirky flair,
Blankets of laughter fill the cool air.

Fireflies twinkle, catch a glow or two,
Winking at dreams, as if they just knew.
Each flicker's a joke, a tiny burst of light,
Sparks of delight all through the night.

In the Embrace of Ancestral Roots

Roots tangled up gossiping below,
Whispers of wisdom, secret and slow.
They chuckle with soil, a humorous crew,
Sharing old stories, just for a few.

Each twist and turn, an ancient jest,
The ground shakes softly, at nature's best.
Who knew the earth held secrets so fun?
Underneath it all, we all are one!

Dialogues with the Wind

The wind whistles tunes, a cheeky breeze,
Pulling my hat off, such a tease!
It tumbles and dances, a playful sprite,
Twisting my hair, oh what a sight!

Talking with whispers, it belly-laughs loud,
Encourages leaves to join in a crowd.
As branches sway, they join the spree,
Nature's own chatter, just wild and free.

Shadows Play on Leafy Layers

In a park where shadows dance,
Squirrels plot a nutty chance.
Cats on branches swoop and dive,
As leaves giggle, come alive.

Sunbeams tickle bark and roots,
While dandelions wear their boots.
A moth flirts, sways on a breeze,
Then bumps into a playful tease.

Dance of the Weathered Leaves

Leaves twirl like dancers bold,
In colors bright, a sight to behold.
They skip and roll from tree to ground,
In a waltz of laughter, joy unbound.

The old oak shakes, does a jig,
While bunnies watch and cheer, so gig.
With each soft rustle, a joke they share,
A riot of fun fills the air!

Majestic Giants of the Glade

Tall and proud, the giants stand,
With knots and grooves like ancient hands.
They whisper tales of years gone by,
While birds swoosh past, oh so spry.

A wise old tree gives a yawn,
As beetles race with the break of dawn.
Belly laughs in nature's choir,
As branches sway, they never tire.

The Language of Acorns

Acorns chatter on the floor,
In secret meetings, they explore.
"What's the gossip?" whispers one,
"I heard the breeze is having fun!"

They roll and tumble, making noise,
As children play with sticks and joys.
A squirrel jokes, "I'm middle-class,"
While they all chuckle, watching grass.

Beneath the Emerald Vault

Under branches wide and bright,
Squirrels dance in morning light.
Tripping over acorns' laugh,
Nature's jest, a playful half.

Rabbits strut with floppy ears,
Tickling roots with giggling sneers.
Whispers from the grassy glade,
Echo jokes the trees have made.

Breath of the Wooden Giants

Twisting trunks, oh what a sight,
Mighty boughs in playful fight.
Ticklish wind, it gives a shove,
Branches giggle, push and shove.

Hiding critters poke their heads,
Waving leaves in leafy beds.
Nature chuckles, sways with glee,
Dancing shadows, wild and free.

Lurking in the Mossy Light

Mossy hats on toadstool heads,
Throwing shade where mischief spreads.
Lizards laugh as they dart and weave,
Sunlight catches what they leave.

Butterflies with silly grins,
Performing tricks where laughter wins.
Every twist a tale to spin,
Nature's comedy begins again.

A Symphony of Rustling Leaves

Leaves are clapping, what a sound,
Nature's band playing all around.
Whistling branches, tapping toes,
For every joke, a giggle flows.

A choir sings in breezy cheer,
Pinecones chuckle, drawing near.
From the ground to sky above,
Trees unite in playful love.

Whispers of the Ancient Grove

In the woods where trees wear crowns,
Squirrels dance and shake their frowns.
Acorns drop like tiny bombs,
Nature's jokes in leafy psalms.

Creaky trunks tell tales of old,
Of a tree that once was bold.
A raccoon here, a fox over there,
Planning schemes without a care.

Branches twitch with cheeky glee,
As the wind plays hide and seek.
Bugs perform a tiny show,
While the moss takes the front row.

Come join the giggles of the glade,
As shadows dance beneath the shade.
In this place where laughter grows,
Every root and branch just knows.

Leaves Beneath the Silent Canopy

Beneath the leaves, a secret's shared,
A chipmunk's laugh, a squirrel dared.
They form a band with sticks and stones,
And dream of jam made from pinecones.

The owl winks, wearing wise old specs,
While rabbits plot their next big checks.
Yet, every whisper comes with glee,
A comedy show for the bumblebee.

Tree trunks turn to gossip queens,
Comparing knots and silly scenes.
Nuts discuss their latest trends,
As the sunlight weaves and bends.

Under the canopy, all is bright,
With laughter echoing left and right.
Forget your worries, dance and play,
Join the fun beneath the sway.

The Heartbeat of Timbered Shadows

In shadows deep where giggles hide,
The bark of laughter does abide.
Woody whispers float and swirl,
While leaves reveal the secrets, twirl.

A deer decides to join the fun,
Twirling 'round till day is done.
While the frogs croak in perfect time,
Creating music with a rhyme.

Branches tickle with a gentle breeze,
As the bugs chant their witty tease.
In a world where silliness flows,
Every moment, pure joy shows.

So rest your head 'neath leafy bed,
Let the giggles fill your head.
Embrace the harmony of cheer,
In the woods, where laughter's near.

Where the Roots Embrace the Earth

A root once asked the dirt, "What's new?"
The dirt replied, "Just growing too!"
With twigs as friends and leaves for capes,
The laughter flows like silly grapes.

The toadstools boast of fancied dreams,
Of knightly quests on mossy beams.
While earthworms wiggle, digging deep,
Softly chuckling, never sleep.

A beetle competes in tiny races,
Leaving behind his silly traces.
The grass can't help but laugh so loud,
At all the antics in the crowd.

So come and root yourself in fun,
In a world where smiles have begun.
With every step, each giggle's worth,
Join the roots that embrace the earth.

Maples and Oaks in Harmony

In the woods where neighbors speak,
A maple joked, 'You're quite unique!'
The oak replied with a sturdy laugh,
'At least I'm not just a sapling's path!'

They shared their shade on summer days,
Admiring each other's leafy ways.
'You sway so graceful, oh mighty friend,'
'But you know my acorns tend to offend!'

Branches Arching in Rapture

The branches danced like limbs of cheer,
'Just watch me bend, I have no fear!'
With a twist and a shout, the elders joked,
'But watch your step or you'll be poked!'

In the breeze, they took their chance,
Swinging wildly like a fun fair dance.
Branches pointing, giggles fly,
'You nearly got a squirrel! Oh my!'

Songs of Seasons Past

Old leaves whisper tales of glee,
Like love notes from a maple tree.
'Back in spring, I had a fling,
But summer's sun made my roots sing!'

With laughter in the autumn air,
They swapped their stories, light as air.
'Leaves falling down—oh, what a show,
Fell for you fast—didn't you know?'

The Gentle Sway of Timeless Trees

Waving gently in the afternoon,
With quiet giggles, they swayed in tune.
'Careful now, don't trip on your bark,
You might just miss a little lark!'

The sun peeked through, a mischievous tease,
As they jived together like a summer breeze.
'With a twist and a turn, let's make a scene,
Who knew we'd be the life of the green?'

A Tapestry of Twisted Branches

In a forest of tangled glee,
Branches doing the cha-cha, can't you see?
Leaves giggle and flutter, what a sight,
Even the squirrels are dancing tonight!

Roots are gossiping under the ground,
Sharing secrets in whispers, so profound.
A parrot in a fancy hat stands near,
Yelling 'Stop, tree-hugging is kinda queer!'

The bark seems to chuckle, wearing a grin,
As beetles play tag, let the games begin!
Even the shadows sway in delight,
A tapestry of laughter, pure and bright.

So come join the fun, let go of your cares,
In this wild woodland, nobody stares.
With branches entwined, together we'll play,
Twisted tales in the trees, hip-hip-hooray!

Sunlight Flickers through Foliage

Sunlight sparkles like a golden coin,
Winking at flowers, playful and joined.
The daisies are gossiping, oh what a show,
While butterflies prance to their dance floor flow.

A sunbeam tickles a cheeky old tree,
Who cracks a joke, 'Are you talking to me?'
Moss claps its hands, the ferns start to sway,
As dappled light winks, come out to play!

Buzzy bees gossip about the best blooms,
While grasshoppers leap as if they've got no rooms.
With shadows and whispers, the lively light plays,
Where sunlight flickers, brightening our days.

So lift up your spirits, dance in the golden,
In this patch of joy, you'll never feel olden.
Let the sunlight tickle, let laughter abound,
In the heart of the woods, pure fun can be found!

The Embrace of Olden Trees

Whispering trunks with stories to share,
Hugging the wind like they just don't care.
With laughter like sap, sweet and alive,
These ancient giants sure know how to thrive.

A squirrel declares he's the king of the wood,
While a raccoon scoffs, saying, 'Ain't that rude?'
Moss-covered knees are aching with joy,
As trees swap tall tales, like a grand old ploy.

Branches intertwine like friends in a brawl,
While shadows stretch out, casting giggles small.
The owls roll their eyes, 'Why don't they all hush?'
As laughter erupts in a jovial rush.

So come hear the whispers from bark that is wise,
Join the fun below the colorful skies.
In the embrace of old friends, as nature believes,
Laughter grows louder among the old trees!

Serenade of the Verdant Veil

Under the canopy, merriment blooms,
With frogs in tuxedos croaking tunes.
The flowers are twirling, a colorful parade,
While a chipmunk conducts from a leafy shade.

A shy little fern tries to steal the show,
With arms wide open, 'Hey, look at me grow!'
The trees lean in closer, straining to see,
As a snail in a top hat exclaims, 'Yippee!'

A chorus of crickets joins the delight,
Making music till the fall of the night.
With each note that echoes in the rich air,
The verdant veil dances, light as a prayer.

So gather your laughter, don't let it stall,
In this serenade, everyone's welcome to call.
With greenery grinning, let the night sway,
To the melody of nature, come out and play!

The Oak's Murmurs

In the shade, squirrels chatter away,
They plot their antics, in sun and in play.
Branches sway, they dance to a tune,
While owls hoot, 'How rude, what a cartoon!'

The tree gives a creak, a whisper so sly,
"Watch out for the bees, don't let them fly by!"
A squirrel nods, with a grin on his face,
He dances and dodges, in this silly race.

Chronicles of the Canopy

High in the branches, the parakeets squawk,
Sharing gossip, while the branches rock.
"Did you see how the raccoon got stuck?"
"He thought it was funny, now he's just out of luck!"

A chipmunk jumps in, with a tale so tall,
"I found a lost acorn, the biggest of all!"
The tree chuckles softly, its bark in a grin,
As the gossip among creatures just circles again.

Dreams of the Forest Floor

Down by the roots, where the mushrooms grow,
A worm tells of tales, with a wiggly glow.
"Did you hear? The fox thought he'd dig a new hole,
But tripped on a beetle, that took quite a toll!"

The daisies giggle, as the breeze starts to tease,
"Why don't you come dance in the soft summer breeze?"
And while the wildflowers sway and they bend,
They burst into laughter, it'll never end!

The Breath of Ancient Wood

The old tree sighs, with wisdom to share,
"Life's like a game, but do we play fair?"
A badger winks, with a cheeky little stance,
"Sure, if you dodge me; it's all just a dance!"

A beetle joins in, with a proud little strut,
"Why walk when we roll? Come on let's cut!"
Laughter echoes under the leafy green dome,
Where every critter is always at home.

A Sonnet for the Tall Ones

In the forest, giants sway and dance,
Each tree a ladder in a slow romance,
Leaves whisper secrets, but just out of reach,
While squirrels plot mischief on the bark's beach.

With roots like anchors, they do not shake,
Yet, in the breeze, they giggle and quake,
A high-five for critters who run with glee,
A ruckus of laughter from branches we see.

Their shadows stretch long, like a winter's sigh,
A canopy woven where time slips by,
Yet when the sun dips, they snort and collapse,
For even tall trees know when to take naps.

So raise a toast to those towering friends,
Who keep us grounded as the daylight ends,
With bark like armor and heart so sincere,
Let's share a giggle, for they know no fear.

Old Souls of the Sylvan Realm

In the glade where the light gets diffused,
The critters are snoozing, a bit overused,
Old owls crack jokes, with a wink and a glare,
As branches break up their not-so-fine hair.

The foxes play poker with deft little paws,
While raccoons plot schemes with not much applause,
They laugh at the sun as it tries to peek through,
Unruly mischief, a merry crew.

Whispers of yesteryear dance in the leaves,
Traditions of acorns that nobody believes,
They focus on fun, while humans just frown,
And giggle with glee as the moon slips down.

So join in the chaos, the nature's delight,
Embrace the old souls that sparkle at night,
For in every chuckle, a story unfolds,
In this sylvan kingdom, where laughter is gold.

The Rustle of Old Pages

In forests vast, where stories arise,
Each tree a tome with curious ties,
The wind turns the pages, and all can see,
Tales of the silly, from birch to the bee.

Covered in moss, the books wear a hat,
Scribbles of squirrels and a wise, old cat,
Whispers of laughter as they share their jest,
Laughter is timeless; it simply won't rest.

The sun paints the margins, the moon gives a wink,
As tales intertwine and make critters think,
Of love and mischief in every bend,
Stories of foolishness that never seem to end.

So open your ears, let nature recite,
For the rustling leaves bring magic to night,
In these ancient pages, fun waits to be found,
In the library living, with laughter profound.

Nature's Embrace

In the glen where the chuckles bloom wide,
The flowers wear laughter like a bright pride,
Bees hum a tune that's perfectly sweet,
As butterflies laugh with their fluttering feet.

The rivers create ripples of ticklish glee,
While mountains stand tall, sipping joy with tea,
The sun plays hopscotch with shadows around,
Painting bright smiles on the ground where we're found.

Dewdrops are giggles that fall from the sky,
While daisies wiggle as the breeze drifts by,
With every embrace, nature weaves a thread,
A tapestry woven from the laughter we've bred.

So savor the joy in this lively space,
For nature's warm hug is a delightful place,
Where whimsy and wonder step into the light,
And every heart dances with pure delight.

The Heartbeat of the Forest

A squirrel struts with pride,
He thinks he's King of the Wood.
Chasing his nutty dreams,
He stumbles, oh, how he's good!

The owls hoot with delight,
And giggle in the night.
Beavers build a dam of puns,
While fish joke about the bite.

A raccoon dreams of fame,
Wearing a leaf for a crown.
Yet tripping on twigs again,
He giggles, won't let down.

So here, all creatures play,
Laughing 'neath the bright sun.
In a world of whimsy,
Each heartbeat is pure fun.

Nightfall under the Foliage

The moon peeks through the trees,
With a giggle in her glow.
Fireflies dance like sparkly thoughts,
In nature's evening show.

A fox plays hide and seek,
With shadows creeping low.
But the turtle takes his time,
Saying slow is how to go.

Bats swoop down with flair,
Chasing moths in silly flight.
While frogs croak rhymes so loud,
Their tunes echo through the night.

Underneath the starry sky,
The woodland's laughter spreads.
In the heart of this wild place,
Big dreams rest on little beds.

Chronicles of the Woodland

Once stood a tree so wise,
With a grin that seemed to tease.
He taught the birds to sing,
And made the breezes freeze.

A rabbit wrote his tale,
With carrots as his pen.
He scribbled down adventures,
Then lost them in the den.

With whispers through the leaves,
The stories weaves all night.
Raccoons gather 'round,
For snacks and lots of bites.

So every creature knows,
In the forest's playful glen,
The chronicles of woodland fun,
Will bring them back again.

Secrets of the Sturdy Boughs

In the branches so robust,
The secrets softly hum.
A family of ants converse,
While dreaming of the sun.

The owls share wisecracks,
Wrapped in a cozy night.
While squirrels eat snacks,
Their giggles take to flight.

A deer sidesteps the plants,
With a wink and playful nose.
Whispering passing jokes,
To any bloom that grows.

So here among the boughs,
Laughter flourishes and glows.
With every rustle and breeze,
The secrets dance like prose.

Reverie Amongst the Roots

Beneath the branches, squirrels prance,
Chasing each other in a silly dance.
The roots, like arms, stretch wide and far,
Whispering secrets beneath the stars.

A raccoon giggles, with mischief abound,
Stealing my sandwich, oh what a hound!
The leaves chuckle, a soft rustling sound,
As nature's laughter echoes around.

In the shade, I ponder, who wears the best hat?
A crow in a beak, or the cat with a spat?
Here in this realm where smiles take flight,
Every creature glimmers, pure delight.

So let's toast to this wood, a whimsical place,
Where laughter and joy have their rightful space.
With each fallen acorn, a giggle is found,
In reverie among the roots, love abounds.

The Silent Sentinel

Standing tall, the tree looks wise,
With knots like wrinkles, and leaves like ties.
A squirrel in uniform, pretending to guard,
Yells 'Halt!' at a breeze that's acting quite hard.

With squirrels on duty, the air is alive,
A secret club where they all can thrive.
They draft silly laws, like no acorns shared,
And only on Tuesdays are naps truly spared.

A bird drops by, a feathered scout,
Chirping a song about a new route.
The sentinel chuckles, though quite still in form,
As laughter's the norm within nature's warm.

With roots deep in laughter and branches of fun,
The silent sentinel watches everyone.
In each silly moment, a wink and a grin,
This tree knows the joy that grows from within.

Echoes in the Timber

In the timber's heart, the woodpecker knocks,
A drummer of nature, in rhythm, he rocks.
The owls roll their eyes, 'Here we go again!'
Taunting the pecker, 'What's wrong with your zen?'

Echoes resound with each playful thud,
As laughter and giggles rise up from the mud.
Tree frogs join in with their chorus of croaks,
While rabbits form jokes that'll leave you in strokes.

A beaver, quite crafty, builds dams made of quips,
To catch all the laughter that drips from their lips.
'When you can't find a giggle, look up or down!'
In the timber's embrace, joy wears a crown.

From branches and boughs, the humor cascades,
In echoes so rich, no laughter evades.
Nature's own jester, this woodland delight,
In echoes and antics, everything's right.

Dreams Woven in Bark

Bark like a tapestry, stories unfold,
Of critters and giggles, and brave tales of old.
A fox tells a yarn, with tail high and proud,
As the mushrooms chuckle, beneath their damp shroud.

Dreams weave together, in knots and in loops,
While ants in a lineup perform silly scoops.
They march with their crumbs, a parade in the glen,
With banners of laughter, they giggle and zen.

A rabbit with glasses reads fables aloud,
While the owls settle in, a thoughtful crowd.
They snicker at puns that weave through the air,
In the world of the forest, there's laughter to share.

In dreams woven tight, beneath canopy's dome,
Every wurly tale feels just like home.
With smiles and chuckles, a fun little lark,
In a forest of dreams, with whimsy in bark.

Shadows of Wisdom in the Glade

In the shade where the squirrels play,
The wise old owl won't come out to say,
He hoots and chuckles, barely awake,
While critters ponder their next nutty take.

Beneath the branches, whispers arise,
A frog jumps high, surprising the flies,
With every croak, he shares a tale,
Of dreams to leap and a wish to sail.

A hedgehog rolls with a sleepy yawn,
Dreaming of lunch, at the break of dawn,
His spiky coat a fashion statement,
In this green realm, he finds contentment.

By the roots, a rabbit lays her claim,
With a wiggle and hop, she joins the game,
In this glade, the fun never ends,
As laughter bubbles among the friends.

Reflections in the Dappled Shade

In the dappled light, the critters dance,
Each shadow shifts with a funny prance,
A squirrel slips on a leafy cap,
As laughter echoes, he takes a nap.

A turtle in shades takes his sweet time,
While mockingbird sings a silly rhyme,
They join in chorus, a quirky pair,
In the shimmering light, without a care.

Butterflies twirl in a pastel hue,
In the flip-flop of fun, they simply flew,
A fairy's giggle fills the afternoon,
As sunbeams twinkle like a silver tune.

In this joyful spot, all worries cease,
Every critter finds a moment of peace,
With chuckles and wit, they simply bask,
In the great green shades, no serious task.

Echoing Footsteps on Leafy Paths

Footsteps crunch on a leafy bed,
A playful raccoon scampers ahead,
He stops and stares, a sly little grin,
As the shadows follow, he winks and spins.

A badger ambles, his belly quite round,
Mumbling secrets in the trees he found,
Each step an echo, a humorous slip,
In the soft leaf cover, he takes a trip.

A rabbit hops by, wearing a hat,
Declares himself king, oh imagine that!
He waves to the ducks, who quack with delight,
In this playful kingdom, everything's right.

With each echoing step, the fun multiplies,
As laughter and giggles fill the skies,
On these leafy paths, joy knows no bounds,
In the heart of the woods, happiness sounds.

The Scent of Earth and Rain

After the storm, the world is fresh,
Worms wiggle out and start a mesh,
A muddy snail says, 'What a day!'
With slime and fun, he slides away.

The grass smells sweet, the puddles shine,
Frogs leap around, feeling divine,
They croak their tunes, a silly refrain,
In the dance of droplets, they feel no pain.

A brave little mouse with a raincoat on,
Dares to explore as the skies have shone,
With each little squish, a giggle escapes,
The woodland fun surely takes shapes.

As the sun emerges, a rainbow glows,
Critters unite for fun in their clothes,
In the scent of earth, they spin and prance,
Celebrating life with a joyful dance.

Guardians of the Green Realm

In the forest where squirrels play,
The guardians dance in a goofy way.
With capes made of leaves, oh what a sight,
They chase their tails and take to flight.

A raccoon wearing glasses gets quite the cheer,
He claims to be wise, but we know he's a deer!
With antics so wild, they laugh and they tease,
In this green kingdom, it's fun with ease.

They hold meetings by moonlight, you see,
Discussing the mysteries of the tall, grand tree.
Yet half the time, they forget what to say,
As laughter erupts, they just call it a day.

So come join the fun, and wear your best grin,
The guardians of green will invite you right in.
With giggles and joy filling up the air,
You'll leave with a smile, without a care!

Reflections in the Trunk

Peek into the trunk, what's hiding right there?
A family of critters in a whimsical lair.
They mirror their fears in the soft, dark wood,
Comical stories that spin in the hood.

A young chipmunk dresses in fabric so bold,
Claims he's an artist with stories untold.
While a wise old owl just hoots with delight,
As the chipmunk begins to sell dreams of the night.

Mirror, mirror, what's true and what's fake?
The trunk chuckles softly, gives a playful shake.
Reflections of nature, kooky and bright,
Build up the silliness, under the moonlight.

In this space so full of life's art,
Every visitor finds a piece of their heart.
With laughter resounding through every small nook,
The trunk holds the joy, just come take a look.

The Poetry of Pollen

In the air, pollen dances with grace,
Tickling the noses of all in the race.
Buzzing around like a tiny parade,
Creating an itch that will not fade.

Bees recite poems, but can't keep a beat,
Stumbling on words, making blunders quite sweet.
Their rhymes get mixed, in a flowery rhyme,
But who can resist this sugary thyme?

The flowers all laugh, what a rambunctious crowd,
As sneezes erupt, the laughter gets loud.
From daisies to dandelions in bloom,
Together they write their own silly tunes.

So raise up your voice, let the sneezes take flight,
Join in the fun, let your joy shine bright.
The poetry of pollen is more than a prance,
It's a whirling, twirling, sneezing romance!

Rustling Stories in the Breeze

The breeze carries tales from the trees up so high,
With whispers and giggles, they flutter and fly.
Each leaf has a secret, a plan or a dream,
Rustling together like a mischievous team.

A branch tells a story of a nut that got lost,
While a squirrel nearby lets out a small cost.
"I found it!" he squeaks, with a leap and a sway,
But the wind just chuckles, "It rolled far away."

The wisps weave together in a playful dance,
Narrating the mischief that leads to romance.
As critters gather round for the tales of the breeze,
They giggle and chirp, with snacks made of cheese.

So lend an ear closely to the rustling sound,
For stories are plenty where joy can be found.
The breeze beckons softly, come join in the cheer,
In a world filled with laughter, there's nothing to fear!

Intertwined Hearts of the Grove

In the grove where squirrels play,
Trees are gossiping away.
Leaves dance in a silly breeze,
Telling jokes, and laughing with ease.

A raccoon juggles acorns fast,
While owls hoot, but not too blast.
The branches twist in playful glee,
Nature's comedy, so wild and free.

Bark bids hello to passing deer,
Says, "Stay and chat, lend me an ear!"
With every rustle, laughter rings,
In this grove, joy's the king of things.

So next time you stroll through the trees,
Listen closely, if you please.
For in the whispers, you'll surely find,
A fun-filled world, so gentle and kind.

The Weaver's Glade

In a glade where spiders spin,
Their webs gleam with a cheeky grin.
A butterfly flutters, thinks it's grand,
While grasshoppers form a quirky band.

The flowers bloom with colors bright,
But bees complain, 'It's just too bright!'
This floral stage of nature's art,
Keeps the critters all playing their part.

A rabbit hops with cotton tail,
Chasing shadows, leaving a trail.
Toads croak jokes that sound quite funny,
As frogs emerge, looking for money.

So wander through, take in the scene,
Where laughter blooms, evergreen.
In this glade, no worries hold,
Just funny tales in whispers told.

Tales Etched in Timber

Carved in bark, secrets do dwell,
Woodpeckers knock, ringing the bell.
Tales of mischief by woodland critters,
Echo between bark and glitter.

The porcupine sings out of tune,
While squirrels search for hidden spoons.
A deer in checkered socks prances by,
Winking under the sunny sky.

Beetles march in a tiny line,
Carrying crumbs, feeling divine.
Fungi giggle in sporadic bursts,
With every poke, it quivers and bursts.

Listen close, if you dare,
To stories told on the woodland air.
For every tree has a jest to share,
In the tales etched here, everywhere!

From Seed to Splendor

A little acorn dreams so big,
Wishing to grow, dance, and jig.
But what it finds as it strives to rise,
Is the antics of critters that surprise.

The sapling laughs at the breeze's tease,
Swaying along with perfectly ease.
A chipmunk rolls right past its feet,
Claiming it's the world's best seat.

As years go by, with roots so deep,
The grand oak stands, no time for sleep.
Yet every now and then, it quakes,
With ticklish winds that give it shakes.

From seed to splendor, it's quite the sight,
Nature's humor, pure delight.
So next time you look at a tree so fair,
Remember the giggles hidden with care.

Footfalls on the Forest Floor

In the woods where critters roam,
I slipped on moss, felt far from home.
A squirrel laughed as I fell down,
Guess I won't win any forest crown.

The trees, they gawked, their branches swayed,
I swear I heard a fern dismay.
Just tripped on roots, all in good fun,
Nature's comedy has just begun.

A chipmunk chuckled, oh what a sight,
He winked at me, then scampered right.
I gathered myself with a sheepish grin,
Who knew that falling could be such a win?

As leaves chuckled in the breeze above,
I danced with trees—oh, what a love!
For every tumble, there's laughter more,
In this forest where joy's at the core.

Nature's Resonance

The winds hum tunes through the tall pines,
They crack jokes in the sun, such lines!
Birds sing back, a sarcastic reply,
Nature's orchestra, oh my, oh my!

A bear strolled by, with a comical pace,
He's got two left feet, a clumsy grace.
The bees all buzz, it sounds like a tease,
In this leafy realm, everyone's a tease.

The brook burbles while rolling its eyes,
Here's where the frogs share their wisecrack lies.
Each ripple laughs, a giggle so sweet,
In Nature's resonance, nothing's discreet!

The plants all sway, their green heads shake,
Telling tall tales that make the ground quake.
In this merry land, life's always a jest,
Come laugh with nature, it's truly the best!

A Chorus of Treefrogs

In the glade, where shadows play,
Treefrogs gather, hip-hip hooray!
With warty skins, they leap and croak,
A concert starts; it's no joke!

They ribbit tunes, a chorus grand,
While fireflies wave their tiny hands.
Each note a prank, oh what a croak,
Even the crickets start to joke!

A toad joins in, trying to steal the show,
But trips on his tongue; oh no, oh no!
The frogs all giggle, a raucous delight,
As night wraps the forest in soft twilight.

Their laughter echoes, a funny refrain,
Mirthful moments that will not wane.
For in this swampy, green-glassed space,
Nature's humor finds its place.

In the Shade of Wisdom

Beneath wise branches, I sat down low,
The leaves whispered secrets, a gentle flow.
An owl winked as he shared his lore,
"Life is better when you snore!"

A squirrel chimed in, with a nutty quip,
"Focus on snacks, take a hearty sip."
The sun peeked in, with a playful glare,
"Don't mind the shadows; they hide all your flair!"

"Embrace your quirks," said a crooked tree,
"Even if you look just like me!"
I chuckled at nature's wise brigade,
Laughter and wisdom, perfectly made.

So in this refuge, I find my cheer,
With each funny thought that brings me near.
In the shade of wisdom, under the sun,
Life and laughter, perfectly spun.

The Resonance of Growth

In the forest where the acorns fall,
Squirrels gather, having a ball.
They chat about the tree's great height,
Claim to wisdom, but none can write.

Roots below tickle the ground,
While branches sway without a sound.
Leaves gossip when the breeze comes by,
Telling tales of the butterflies.

Rain drips down like laughter's cheer,
Each drop a song, oh so clear.
Trees chuckle softly, don't take a stance,
Yet invite all creatures to join the dance.

Wisdom grows with every sprout,
Claiming knowledge without a doubt.
And when the sun sets on this show,
The trees just laugh—they're still in the know.

Silent Allies of the Understory

In the shadow where the ferns reside,
Whispers travel with the tide.
The mushrooms plot a daring scene,
While the toadstools wear a cap so green.

Snails debate their slow-paced race,
While beetles dance in a festive space.
Every critter hides from giant feet,
And crickets chime a rhythmic beat.

In the cool of the dirt, secrets unfold,
As roots tell stories that can't be sold.
"I swear I saw an ant wear a hat!"
The gossip spreads, imagine that!

Laughter echoes 'neath the weighty leaves,
In the stillness, everyone believes.
For those in the understory play their part,
Silly and wise, each with a heart.

The Starlit Canopy

Above our heads like a joyful maze,
Stars twinkle down in mischievous ways.
"Catch me!" they seem to tease and flit,
While owls compete in an expert wit.

The branches sway, a grand charade,
Moonlight glimmers, the night parade.
Bats swoop low, with playful zoom,
Eclipsing moths in their costume gloom.

The trees hold court, so regal and grand,
With raccoons as jesters, all perfectly planned.
"Who's the brightest?" the stars do ask,
While the fireflies flash, a glowing task.

These heights are not just for solemn dreams,
But a canvas for laughter, or so it seems.
What a show, what a sight to see,
Under the starlit canopy, oh me!

Moonlight on Weathered Bark

As the moon spills its silver light,
Old trees chuckle, feeling quite bright.
Their bark tells tales of years gone past,
With grooves and lines, it's a spell they cast.

Raccoons dance on their sturdy floor,
Their antics leave us begging for more.
"Hey, look at me!" one proudly shouts,
While the owl hoots in wise doubts.

Lichens giggle, painting smiles,
Covering trunks with colorful styles.
"Call us your nature's art," they plea,
With a wink so sly, oh can't you see?

In moonlight's glow, mischief brews,
With trees as hosts, they have much to lose.
For under their watch, hilarity sparks,
Beneath the magic of weathered bark.

A Tapestry of Twists and Turns

In a forest where socks seem to vanish,
The squirrels wear them, oh what a banish!
A raccoon with a hat, so dapper and fine,
He juggles the acorns, a sight so divine.

The trees gossip low, with branches that sway,
They tell tales of critters who've lost their way.
A fox in a suit, he dances with flair,
While a hedgehog recites a poem mid-air.

Around every turn, there's a giggle or two,
A jumping toad sings in his favorite hue.
While wise owls debate on the best kind of cheese,
The laughter of leaves joins the fun in the breeze.

So skip through the trails, where whimsy is king,
Embrace every twist that the nature can bring.
For in every nook, there's a jest waiting there,
In this tapestry woven, pure joy fills the air.

Mysteries of the Knotted Roots

Beneath the gnarled trees, secrets reside,
Where roots twist and tangle, like paths that divide.
A beetle in glasses, he studies the ground,
As whispers of frogs make a comical sound.

A mouse in a cape oversees his domain,
While daring young rabbits play tag in the rain.
The shadows grow longer as twilight descends,
The trees chuckle softly, like long-lost friends.

With roots that are knotted, and tales full of cheer,
They pull up their socks and sing songs to the deer.
Each mystery learned is a laugh to behold,
In the forest where havoc and humor unfold.

So search for the pot where the giggles do brew,
In knots of confusion, there's laughter for you.
For under each wrinkle of nature's own heart,
A funny surprise waits, a delightful work of art.

The Cradle of Forgotten Fables

In the cradle of trees, where stories were spun,
Lies a tale of a turtle who thought he could run.
He challenged a rabbit, who giggled with glee,
Only to nap 'neath a shade—oh, the irony!

An old owl recites a fable of yore,
Of a porcupine stuck in a revolving door.
With quills all a-flutter, he danced the wrong jig,
While the critters all laughed at his hilarious dig.

From squirrels who prance to the turtles who tease,
The tales get more wild with each rustling breeze.
The cradle rocks softly, and echoes the fun,
Forgotten fables turn into laughter's bright sun.

So gather around where the tales come alive,
In a cradle of legends, humor will thrive.
For every old fable, with laughter it weaves,
A tapestry of joy that the forest believes.

Dappled Dreams Beneath an Open Sky

Under the branches where shadows dance light,
A troupe of ants plans a picnic tonight.
With crumbs from a sandwich, a feast is in sight,
While a ladybug dances, oh what a delight!

The sunbeams come down, like confetti on grass,
As squirrels play tag while the shadows all pass.
The grasshoppers serenade with a tune,
While butterflies join with a glowing maroon.

In this dappled dream, where the echoes all play,
A frog in a tiara just won't hop away.
He croaks out the chorus; the breezes applaud,
As the daisies all giggle, it's really quite odd.

So wander through wonders beneath skies so vast,
In dappled dreams where the smiles hold fast.
For every laugh mingled beneath that bright hue,
Is a tapestry woven for each one of you.

Talking to the Wind through Branches

I shouted to the wind, so free,
It whispered back, 'Just let me be!'
The branches creaked, a laughing tree,
They told my secrets with such glee.

I asked the leaves for a good joke,
They rustled softly, then they broke.
A squirrel giggled, in yoga pose,
While I just stood there, struck by prose.

The breeze then teased, 'You seem confused!'
I pondered on the words, bemused.
But as I listened, I had to grin,
Those silly branches had me in!

So here I stand with nature's pals,
In leafy whispers and breezy gales.
Next time I chat with wind, I swear,
I'll bring some snacks, have more to share!

Lanterns of Gold in the Autumn Glade

In the autumn glade, the leaves turn bright,
Like lanterns of gold, a pretty sight.
I found a mushroom in a neat bow tie,
It winked at me, oh my! Oh my!

The squirrels were throwing a nutty feast,
As birds gave speeches, they never ceased.
One crow asked, 'Who's the funniest here?'
The leaf replied, 'It's you, my dear!'

A raccoon danced, he tripped on a root,
The leaves erupted with joyous hoot!
The acorns rolled, they joined the fun,
Singing songs of autumn, one by one.

Just when I thought I'd seen it all,
A fox in socks began to crawl.
In this gold-lit glade where laughter roams,
Nature's jesters have found their homes!

Whispers of the Ancient Grove

The ancient grove with wisdom rich,
Is home to a talking, wise old witch.
She brewed her tea with leaves and bark,
While owls delivered jokes after dark.

The trees would chuckle, their trunks would shake,
As every creature woke with a quake.
A bunny joked, 'Is it tea-time yet?'
The witch replied, 'Only if you bet!'

The shadows giggled, the breezes laughed,
In nature's joke book, a tiny draft.
With whispers shared from bark to stone,
I joined their laughter, never alone.

So when the moon rises high and wide,
The grove unveils its funny side.
In whispers soft, they all agree,
Laughter's the best way to be free!

Beneath the Canopy of Time

Beneath the great, eternal shade,
Time takes a nap, a lovely trade.
The ants held court to bring some cheer,
While crickets serenade from near.

A turtle sighed, 'I'm feeling fast,'
The fickle winds just blew and passed.
They played hide and seek, oh what a feat,
While I just sat with my tired feet.

The branches swayed, gossip all around,
They shared the tales of lost and found.
Mossy carpets chuckled, 'Life's a show!'
With every tick, the antics grow.

So here I lay, a time-travel guest,
In laughter's arms, I find my rest.
Beneath the leafy, timeless rhyme,
Everything's funny—what a climb!

Canopies of Hope

Under the leaves, squirrels conspire,
Planning a raid on the bird feeder's fire.
With nuts in their cheeks, they plot and they scheme,
While birds chirp away, lost deep in their dream.

The branches above hold secrets untold,
Worn shoes hang like trophies, so rugged and bold.
A raccoon with style, in sunglasses, he strolls,
Declaring to all that he's found all the moles.

Beneath the thick shade, the cool breezes play,
A picnic is formed, but the ants have their way.
They march in a line, with a crumb on their backs,
While kids laugh and giggle, plotting their snacks.

As dusk falls around, fireflies start to blink,
They twirl in the air, as if dancing in sync.
With dances so silly, the trees seem to sway,
In a world of green laughter, we wish to stay.

Beneath the Boughs

Beneath all the branches, the stories unfold,
Of picnic mishaps and more antics to hold.
A sandwich was tossed, and a dog chased the cat,
Oh, the chaos that follows a squirrel and a hat!

Woodpeckers tap on the trunk, loud and clear,
While wise old owls try to nap without fear.
A rabbit takes charge, waving arms in the air,
Demanding more treats, with a glance of despair.

The shadows grow long, as the sun slips away,
In the twilight glow, all the critters will play.
In a game of tag, with a dash and a leap,
Laughter in echoes, the forest won't sleep.

So gather your friends, bring a laugh and a cheer,
'Neath the boughs of the trees, there's nothing to fear.
With stories and giggles, a night just begun,
In a realm of pure joy, we'll bask in the fun.

Spirits Gather

In a circle of green, the spirits convene,
With whispers of laughter and moments unseen.
A fox with a grin and a hat of bright red,
Speaks tales of the mischief that follows the bread.

The spirits are playful, like shadows in dance,
A raccoon with charm takes his chance for romance.
With a wink at the moon and a twirl of his tail,
He wades through the brambles with a yeti-like wail.

From the roots of the trees, to the tippy-topped pine,
Ghosts of the forest in costumes divine.
They prank all the owls who hoot in surprise,
As the laughter of rustling leaves fills the skies.

So gather around for this whimsical show,
With spirits of nature who put on a glow.
In the heart of the woods, where the funny abounds,
The gathering of laughter is truly profound.

Legacy of the Leaf

A leaf fell from high, with a wink and a spin,
It landed on heads, like a soft, leafy grin.
It danced down the path, making everyone stare,
As a gust of fresh wind blew it back in the air.

Beneath the grand trees, the shadows were thick,
A turtle in specs read a book, what a trick!
While frogs drummed away, with enthusiasm wide,
In a chorus of giggles, no secret to hide.

The legacy spreads, among mushrooms and grass,
Where rabbits hold meetings and turtles all pass.
With plans to build castles from acorns and twine,
They chuckle at all the things left behind.

So cherish the leaf that made laughter take flight,
In the heart of the woods, where the fun feels just right.
In the legacy shared, let the memories weave,
A tapestry bright, from each fluttering leaf.

The Dance of Green Shadows

In the glade where the sunlight meets shadows at play,
The critters unite for a wild cabaret.
With waltzes and jigs, it's a sight to behold,
As insects bring music, with stories retold.

A hedgehog in tights leads a line of fine ants,
As they boogie and shuffle in their fanciful pants.
The grasshoppers croon, soaring high on a breeze,
All while the sweet daisies sway with such ease.

As the sun starts to dip, the dance steps get wild,
A sheepish young rabbit breaks out with a smile.
He twirls on his toes, while the owls give a cheer,
For the dance of the shadows fills all hearts with cheer.

So join in the fun, let your worries all fade,
In the dance of green shadows, where laughter is made.
With each little hop, and a jig in the night,
The forest remembers, in pure, joyful light.

Guardians of the Wildwood

In the forest, squirrels prance,
Chasing shadows with a dance.
A wise old owl watches with a grin,
Laughing softly, 'Where to begin?'

A rabbit hops, a turtle strolls,
While raccoons play hide and roll.
They bicker over who's the best,
But all agree; it's quite the jest!

Beneath the trees, a party brews,
With acorns serving as the dues.
The pinecone band begins to play,
As critters join in pure ballet!

But when the dusk paints skies with gold,
These merry friends will soon grow old.
So here's a toast, raise paw and claw,
To guardians of the wildwood—flaw!

The Dance of the Lasting Leaves

Leaves are swirling, twirling around,
A leafy conga, a colorful sound.
They giggle and spin through the autumn air,
Waltzing with whispers and little flair.

One leaf took a leap and went 'Wheee!',
While others groaned, 'Just let it be!'
In circles and spirals, they twirled so high,
Until a gust sent them up to the sky!

Now they flopped on the ground with a thud,
Creating a ruckus—such a big bud!
They chuckled aloud, in unison cheer,
'Let's do that again, come back next year!'

So each autumn, they practice their moves,
In silly formations, with nothing to lose!
For when you're just leaves, it's all just a game,
As seasons change, they'll still stake their claim!

Verses of the Verdant

In the meadow, grasshoppers sing,
Riveting tunes on each tiny wing.
Nearby, a snail decided to race,
But always lost in the wild chase!

Dandelions laugh, they're quite the jest,
Tickling the bees—'We're the best!'
Butterflies flutter, with colors galore,
While flowers compete to open their core.

A frog jumps up, croaks a sweet beat,
'Come join my band; let's make it neat!'
But all the bugs just sway and groove,
While ants march past with steadfast moves.

Yet stars above watch the scene with glee,
As nature's performance unfolds with esprit.
For in this green world, laughter will reign,
In verses of verdant, life's merry refrain!

Collage of Core and Canopy

The trees make a hat of leafy delight,
Creatures scurry, from morning to night.
Chipmunks chatter with comedic flair,
While owls roll eyes from their lofty lair.

In twilight's glow, shadows stretch long,
As frogs in the pond sing silly songs.
They croak out rhymes, a nature's delight,
Making critters laugh until the night.

Worms dig deep, and tease with a smile,
'We're the champions of our own style!'
While beetles parade with sparkly shells,
Each claiming tales of magical spells.

With humor alive from root to the bow,
Nature's collage in laughter will grow.
For in this world, where whimsy lives free,
The core and canopy sing with glee!

www.ingramcontent.com/pod-product-compliance
Lightning Source LLC
Chambersburg PA
CBHW071818160426
43209CB00003B/131